THE EUGÉNIE ROCHEROLLE SERIES

Intermediate Piano Duet

Christmas Together

6 Piano Duets Arranged by Eugénie Rocherolle

T0085668

Contents

ISBN 978-1-4768-1500-8

HAL•LEONARD®
CORPORATION

7777 W. BLUEMOUND RD. P.O. BOX 13819 MILWAUKEE, WI 53213

Visit Hal Leonard Online at
www.halleonard.com

BLUE CHRISTMAS

SECONDO

Words and Music by BILLY HAYES
and JAY JOHNSON
Arranged by Eugénie Rocherolle

BLUE CHRISTMAS

PRIMO

Words and Music by BILLY HAYES
and JAY JOHNSON
Arranged by Eugénie Rocherolle

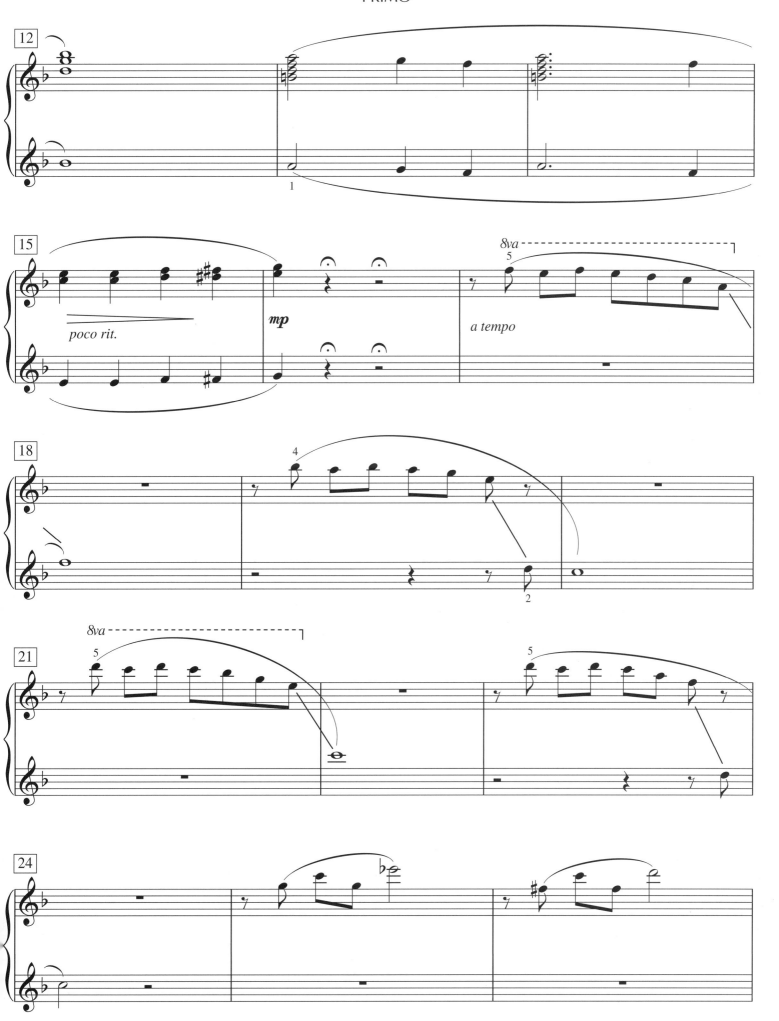

SECONDO

*Repeat optional

PRIMO

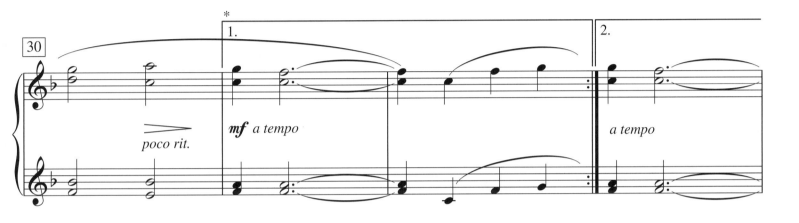

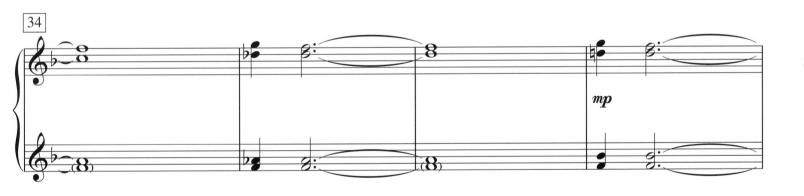

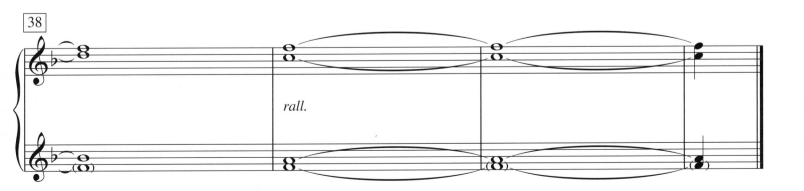

*Repeat optional

THE CHRISTMAS SONG
(Chestnuts Roasting on an Open Fire)

SECONDO

Music and Lyric by MEL TORMÉ
and ROBERT WELLS
Arranged by Eugénie Rocherolle

THE CHRISTMAS SONG
(Chestnuts Roasting on an Open Fire)

PRIMO

Music and Lyric by MEL TORMÉ
and ROBERT WELLS
Arranged by Eugénie Rocherolle

SECONDO

PRIMO

SECONDO

RUDOLPH THE RED-NOSED REINDEER

SECONDO

Music and Lyrics by
JOHNNY MARKS
Arranged by Eugénie Rocherolle

RUDOLPH THE RED-NOSED REINDEER

PRIMO

Music and Lyrics by
JOHNNY MARKS
Arranged by Eugénie Rocherolle

SECONDO

PRIMO

poco rit.   *mp* *a tempo*

PRIMO

SANTA BABY

SECONDO

By JOAN JAVITS,
PHIL SPRINGER and TONY SPRINGER
Arranged by Eugénie Rocherolle

SANTA BABY

PRIMO

By JOAN JAVITS,
PHIL SPRINGER and TONY SPRINGER
Arranged by Eugénie Rocherolle

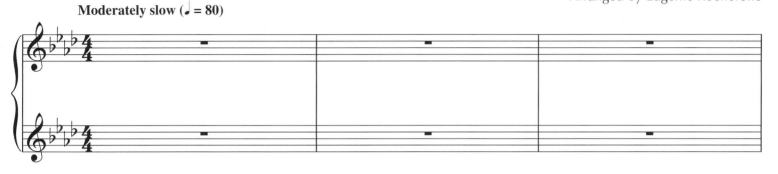

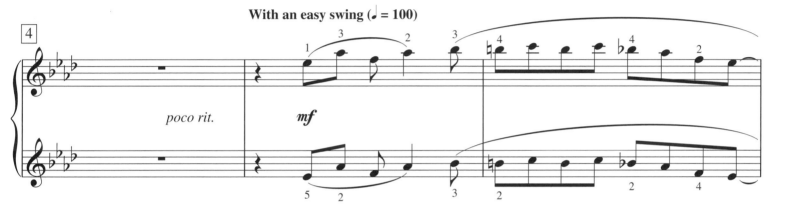

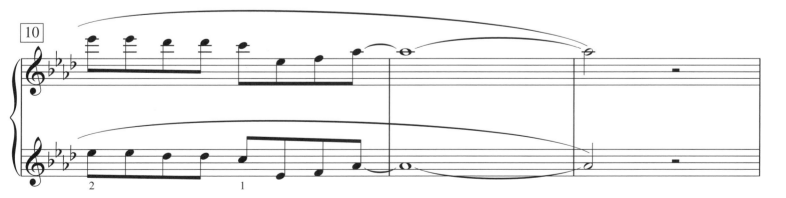

SECONDO

SECONDO

PRIMO

UP ON THE HOUSETOP

SECONDO

Words and Music by B.R. HANBY
Arranged by Eugénie Rocherolle

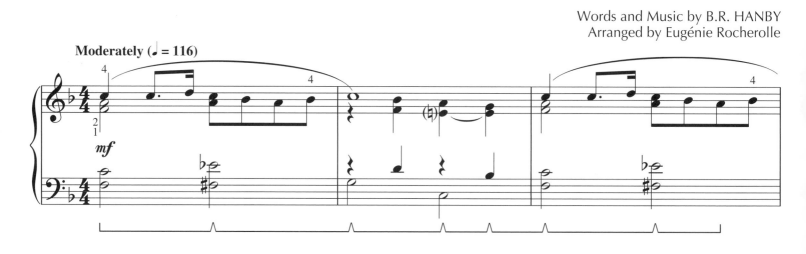

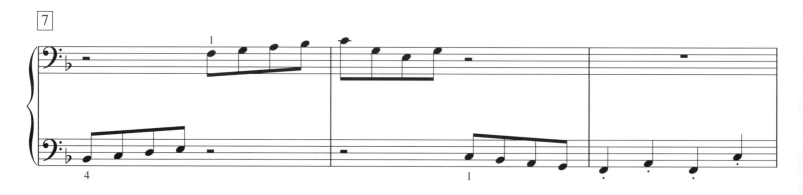

UP ON THE HOUSETOP

PRIMO

Words and Music by B.R. HANBY
Arranged by Eugénie Rocherolle

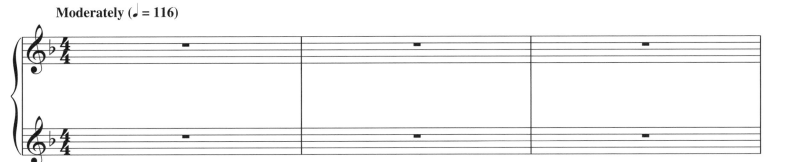

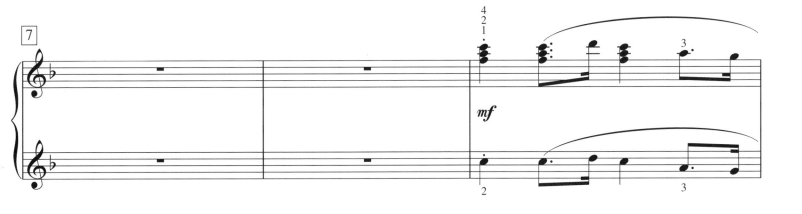

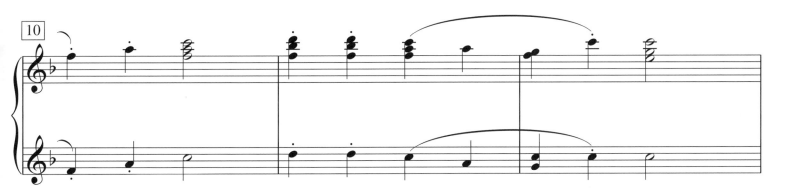

SECONDO

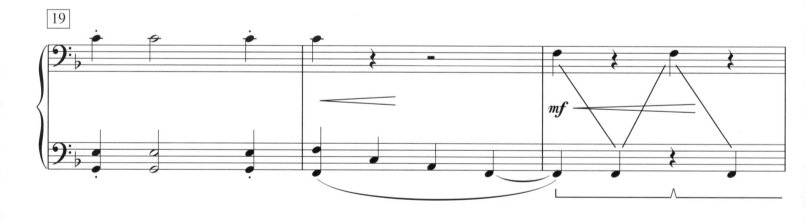

PRIMO

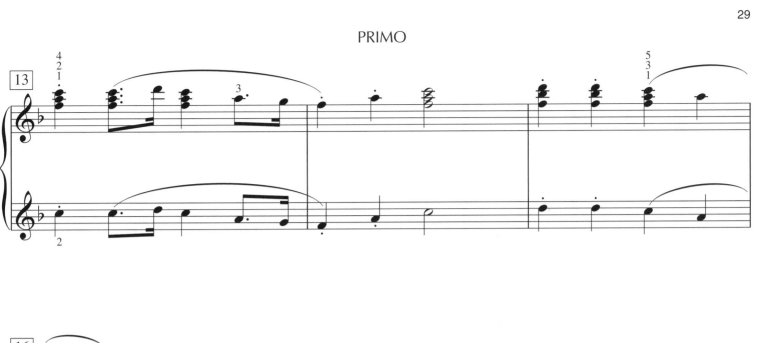

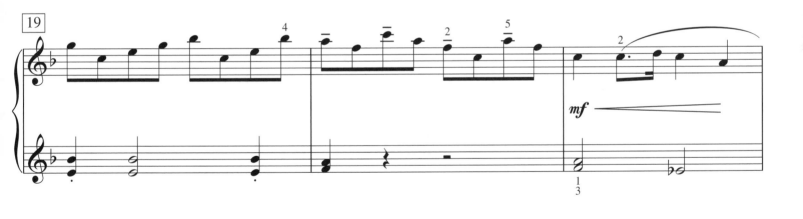

SECONDO

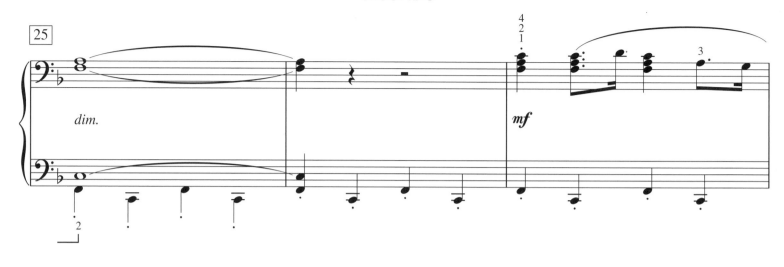

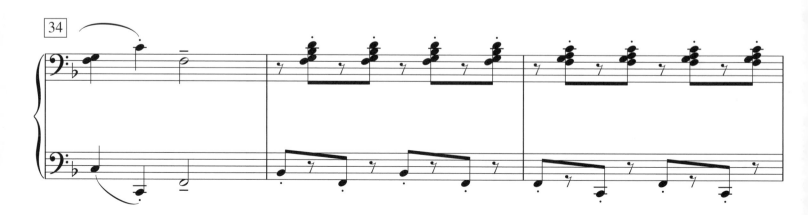

PRIMO

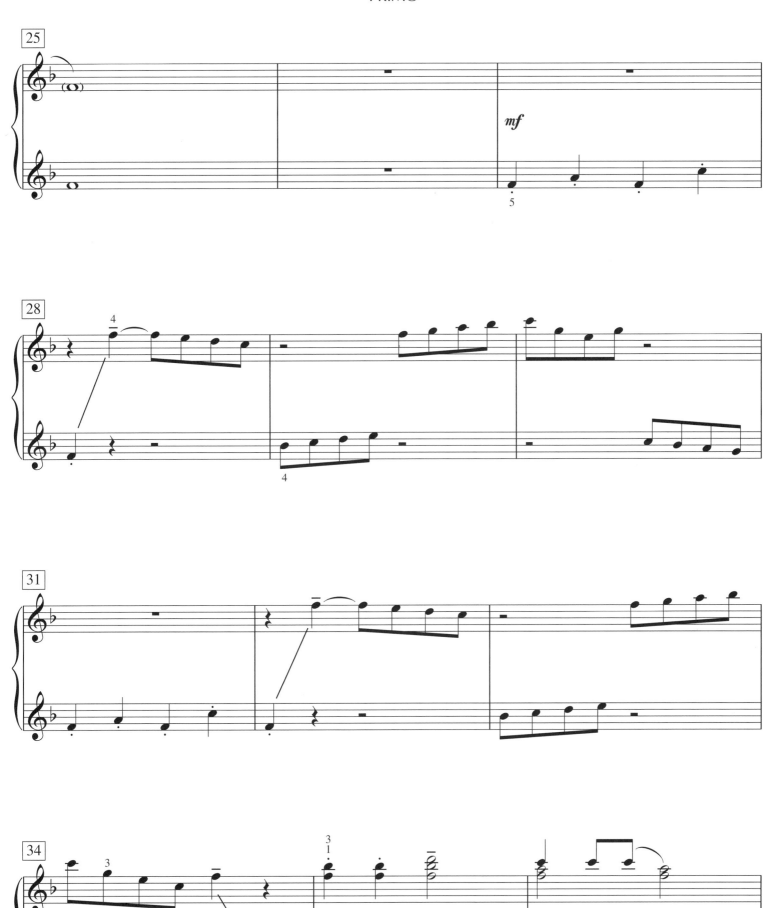

32

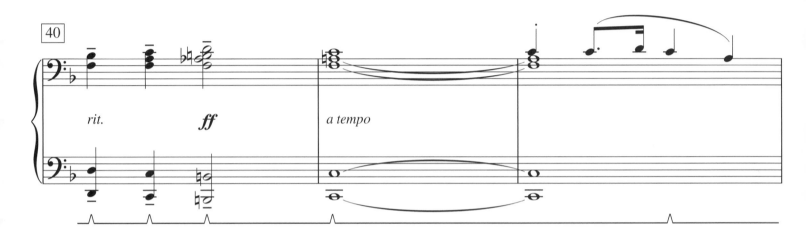

PRIMO

WE WISH YOU A MERRY CHRISTMAS

SECONDO

Traditional English Folksong
Arranged by Eugénie Rocherolle

WE WISH YOU A MERRY CHRISTMAS

PRIMO

Traditional English Folksong
Arranged by Eugénie Rocherolle

SECONDO

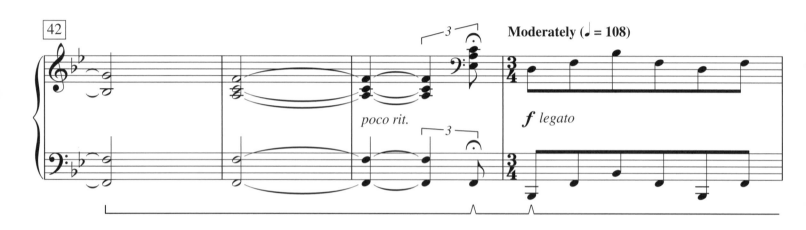

THE EUGÉNIE ROCHEROLLE SERIES

Offering both original compositions and popular arrangements, these stunning collections are ideal for intermediate-level pianists! Each book includes a companion CD with recordings performed by Ms. Rocherolle.

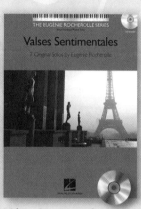

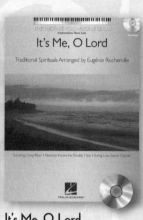

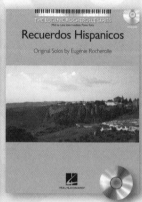

Candlelight Christmas
Eight traditional carols: Away in a Manger • Coventry Carol • Joseph Dearest, Joseph Mine • O Holy Night (duet) • O Little Town of Bethlehem • Silent Night • The Sleep of the Infant Jesus • What Child Is This?
00311808.........................$14.99

Continental Suite
Enjoy the wonders of Europe through these six original piano solos at the intermediate level: Belgian Lace • In Old Vienna • La Piazza • Les Avenues De Paris • Oktoberfest • Rondo Capichio.
00312111 ....$12.99

Valses Sentimentales
Seven original solos: Bal Masque (Masked Ball) • Jardin de Thé (Tea Garden) • Le Long du Boulevard (Along the Boulevard) • Marché aux Fleurs (Flower Market) • Nuit sans Etoiles (Night Without Stars) • Palais Royale (Royal Palace) • Promenade á Deux (Strolling Together).
00311497.........................$12.95

It's Me, O Lord
Nine traditional spirituals: Deep River • It's Me, O Lord • Nobody Knows De Trouble I See • Swing Low, Sweet Chariot • and more.
00311368.........................$12.95

Recuerdos Hispanicos
Seven original solos: Brisas Isleñas (Island Breezes) • Dia de Fiesta (Holiday) • Un Amor Quebrado (A Lost Love) • Resonancias de España (Echoes of Spain) • Niña Bonita (Pretty Girl) • Fantasia del Mambo (Mambo Fantasy) • Cuentos del Matador (Tales of the Matador).
00311369.........................$12.95

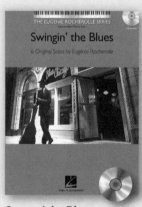

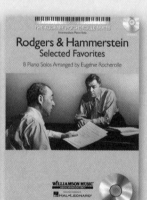

Swingin' the Blues
Six blues originals: Back Street Blues • Big Shot Blues • Easy Walkin' Blues • Hometown Blues • Late Night Blues • Two-Way Blues.
00311445.........................$12.95

Classic Jazz Standards
Ten beloved tunes: Blue Skies • Georgia on My Mind • Isn't It Romantic? • Lazy River • The Nearness of You • On the Sunny Side of the Street • Stardust • Stormy Weather • and more.
00311424.........................$12.95

Rodgers & Hammerstein Selected Favorites
Exquisite, intermediate-level piano solo arrangements of eight favorites from these beloved composers: Climb Ev'ry Mountain • Do-Re-Mi • If I Loved You • Oklahoma • Shall We Dance? • Some Enchanted Evening • There Is Nothin' like a Dame • You'll Never Walk Alone. Includes a CD of Eugénie performing each song.
00311928.........................$14.99

Two's Company
Eugénie Rocherolle gives us a charming and whimsical collection of five original piano duets written for the intermediate-level pianist. The CD includes a recording by Rocherolle of the duet, primo and secondo tracks allowing the performer to practice along with the CD. Duets include: Island Holiday • La Danza • Mood in Blue • Postcript • Whimsical Waltz.
00311883 ....$12.99

On the Jazzy Side
Six delightful jazz piano solos composed by Rocherolle, with her recordings of each on the enclosed CD! Songs: High Five! • Jubilation! • Prime Time • Small Talk • Small Town Blues • Travelin' Light.
00311982.........................$12.99

0212